THE PAIN YOU FEEL

TODAY

is the strength

YOU FEEL TOMORROW

NEVER GIVE UP!

**YOU
CANCER**

FUCKIN APPOINTMENTS I MUST KEEP

	Monday	Tuesday	Wednesday	Thursday	Friday	Saturday	Sunday
WEEK ONE							
WEEK TWO							
WEEK THREE							
WEEK FOUR							

DATES TO REMEMBER

Date	Event	Date	Event	Date	Event

FUCK YOU CANCER MEDICATIONS
(ONE DAY I WANT NEED THIS SHIT)

Medication: _____   Dosage: _____   Frequency: _____
Purpose: _____
Possible Side Effects: _____
_____

Medication: _____   Dosage: _____   Frequency: _____
Purpose: _____
Possible Side Effects: _____
_____

Medication: _____   Dosage: _____   Frequency: _____
Purpose: _____
Possible Side Effects: _____
_____

Medication: _____   Dosage: _____   Frequency: _____
Purpose: _____
Possible Side Effects: _____
_____

Medication: _____   Dosage: _____   Frequency: _____
Purpose: _____
Possible Side Effects: _____
_____

Medication: _____   Dosage: _____   Frequency: _____
Purpose: _____
Possible Side Effects: _____
_____

Medication: _____   Dosage: _____   Frequency: _____
Purpose: _____
Possible Side Effects: _____
_____

Medication: _____   Dosage: _____   Frequency: _____
Purpose: _____
Possible Side Effects: _____

DAMN CONTACT INFO

DOCTORS

POSITION	NAME	PHONE	EMAIL

PHARMACIES, HOSPITALS, AND CLINICS

NAME	PHONE	ADDRESS

PERSONAL SUPPORT

NAME	RELATION	PHONE	EMAIL

BITCH ASS SYMPTOMS AND SIDE EFFECTS

Date	Time	Duration	Description

YOU
CANCER

YOU CANCER

YOU CANCER

YOU
CANCER

**YOU
CANCER**

YOU CANCER

YOU CANCER

YOU CANCER

YOU
CANCER

**YOU
CANCER**

**YOU
CANCER**

YOU CANCER

YOU CANCER

YOU CANCER

**YOU
CANCER**

YOU CANCER

YOU CANCER

YOU
CANCER

**YOU
CANCER**

**YOU CANCER**

FUCKIN APPOINTMENTS I MUST KEEP

	Monday	Tuesday	Wednesday	Thursday	Friday	Saturday	Sunday
WEEK ONE							

	Monday	Tuesday	Wednesday	Thursday	Friday	Saturday	Sunday
WEEK TWO							

	Monday	Tuesday	Wednesday	Thursday	Friday	Saturday	Sunday
WEEK THREE							

	Monday	Tuesday	Wednesday	Thursday	Friday	Saturday	Sunday
WEEK FOUR							

DATES TO REMEMBER

Date	Event	Date	Event	Date	Event

FUCKIN APPOINTMENTS I MUST KEEP

	Monday	Tuesday	Wednesday	Thursday	Friday	Saturday	Sunday
WEEK ONE							
WEEK TWO							
WEEK THREE							
WEEK FOUR							

DATES TO REMEMBER

Date	Event	Date	Event	Date	Event

YOU CANCER

FUCKIN APPOINTMENTS I MUST KEEP

	Monday	Tuesday	Wednesday	Thursday	Friday	Saturday	Sunday
WEEK ONE							

WEEK TWO							

WEEK THREE							

WEEK FOUR							

DATES TO REMEMBER

Date	Event	Date	Event	Date	Event

FUCKIN APPOINTMENTS I MUST KEEP

	Monday	Tuesday	Wednesday	Thursday	Friday	Saturday	Sunday
WEEK ONE							
WEEK TWO							
WEEK THREE							
WEEK FOUR							

DATES TO REMEMBER

Date	Event	Date	Event	Date	Event

 **YOU**
CANCER

FUCKIN APPOINTMENTS I MUST KEEP

	Monday	Tuesday	Wednesday	Thursday	Friday	Saturday	Sunday
WEEK ONE							

WEEK TWO							

WEEK THREE							

WEEK FOUR							

DATES TO REMEMBER

Date	Event	Date	Event	Date	Event

FUCK YOU CANCER MEDICATIONS
(ONE DAY I WANT NEED THIS SHIT)

Medication: _____ Dosage: _____ Frequency: _____
Purpose: _____
Possible Side Effects: _____

Medication: _____ Dosage: _____ Frequency: _____
Purpose: _____
Possible Side Effects: _____

Medication: _____ Dosage: _____ Frequency: _____
Purpose: _____
Possible Side Effects: _____

Medication: _____ Dosage: _____ Frequency: _____
Purpose: _____
Possible Side Effects: _____

Medication: _____ Dosage: _____ Frequency: _____
Purpose: _____
Possible Side Effects: _____

Medication: _____ Dosage: _____ Frequency: _____
Purpose: _____
Possible Side Effects: _____

Medication: _____ Dosage: _____ Frequency: _____
Purpose: _____
Possible Side Effects: _____

Medication: _____ Dosage: _____ Frequency: _____
Purpose: _____
Possible Side Effects: _____

FUCK YOU CANCER MEDICATIONS

(ONE DAY I WANT NEED THIS SHIT)

Medication: _____ Dosage: _____ Frequency: _____

Purpose: _____

Possible Side Effects: _____

Medication: _____ Dosage: _____ Frequency: _____

Purpose: _____

Possible Side Effects: _____

Medication: _____ Dosage: _____ Frequency: _____

Purpose: _____

Possible Side Effects: _____

Medication: _____ Dosage: _____ Frequency: _____

Purpose: _____

Possible Side Effects: _____

Medication: _____ Dosage: _____ Frequency: _____

Purpose: _____

Possible Side Effects: _____

Medication: _____ Dosage: _____ Frequency: _____

Purpose: _____

Possible Side Effects: _____

Medication: _____ Dosage: _____ Frequency: _____

Purpose: _____

Possible Side Effects: _____

Medication: _____ Dosage: _____ Frequency: _____

Purpose: _____

Possible Side Effects: _____

FUCK YOU CANCER MEDICATIONS
(ONE DAY I WANT NEED THIS SHIT)

Medication: _____ Dosage: _____ Frequency: _____
Purpose: _____
Possible Side Effects: _____

Medication: _____ Dosage: _____ Frequency: _____
Purpose: _____
Possible Side Effects: _____

Medication: _____ Dosage: _____ Frequency: _____
Purpose: _____
Possible Side Effects: _____

Medication: _____ Dosage: _____ Frequency: _____
Purpose: _____
Possible Side Effects: _____

Medication: _____ Dosage: _____ Frequency: _____
Purpose: _____
Possible Side Effects: _____

Medication: _____ Dosage: _____ Frequency: _____
Purpose: _____
Possible Side Effects: _____

Medication: _____ Dosage: _____ Frequency: _____
Purpose: _____
Possible Side Effects: _____

Medication: _____ Dosage: _____ Frequency: _____
Purpose: _____
Possible Side Effects: _____

FUCK YOU CANCER MEDICATIONS
(ONE DAY I WANT NEED THIS SHIT)

Medication: _____ Dosage: _____ Frequency: _____
Purpose: _____
Possible Side Effects: _____

Medication: _____ Dosage: _____ Frequency: _____
Purpose: _____
Possible Side Effects: _____

Medication: _____ Dosage: _____ Frequency: _____
Purpose: _____
Possible Side Effects: _____

Medication: _____ Dosage: _____ Frequency: _____
Purpose: _____
Possible Side Effects: _____

Medication: _____ Dosage: _____ Frequency: _____
Purpose: _____
Possible Side Effects: _____

Medication: _____ Dosage: _____ Frequency: _____
Purpose: _____
Possible Side Effects: _____

Medication: _____ Dosage: _____ Frequency: _____
Purpose: _____
Possible Side Effects: _____

Medication: _____ Dosage: _____ Frequency: _____
Purpose: _____
Possible Side Effects: _____

DAMN CONTACT INFO

DOCTORS

POSITION	NAME	PHONE	EMAIL

PHARMACIES, HOSPITALS, AND CLINICS

NAME	PHONE	ADDRESS

PERSONAL SUPPORT

NAME	RELATION	PHONE	EMAIL

YOU CANCER

DAMN CONTACT INFO

DOCTORS

POSITION	NAME	PHONE	EMAIL

PHARMACIES, HOSPITALS, AND CLINICS

NAME	PHONE	ADDRESS

PERSONAL SUPPORT

NAME	RELATION	PHONE	EMAIL

DAMN CONTACT INFO

DOCTORS

POSITION	NAME	PHONE	EMAIL

PHARMACIES, HOSPITALS, AND CLINICS

NAME	PHONE	ADDRESS

PERSONAL SUPPORT

NAME	RELATION	PHONE	EMAIL

DAMN CONTACT INFO

DOCTORS

POSITION	NAME	PHONE	EMAIL

PHARMACIES, HOSPITALS, AND CLINICS

NAME	PHONE	ADDRESS

PERSONAL SUPPORT

NAME	RELATION	PHONE	EMAIL

BITCH ASS SYMPTOMS AND SIDE EFFECTS

Date	Time	Duration	Description

BITCH ASS SYMPTOMS AND SIDE EFFECTS

Date	Time	Duration	Description

BITCH ASS SYMPTOMS AND SIDE EFFECTS

Date	Time	Duration	Description

BITCH ASS SYMPTOMS AND SIDE EFFECTS

Date	Time	Duration	Description

BITCH ASS SYMPTOMS AND SIDE EFFECTS

Date	Time	Duration	Description

Made in the USA
Monee, IL
19 October 2023

44810456R00083